Elephants

ABDO
Publishing Company

A Buddy Book
by
Julie Murray

VISIT US AT
www.abdopub.com

Published by Buddy Books, an imprint of ABDO Publishing Company, 4940 Viking Drive, Suite 622, Edina, Minnesota 55435. Copyright © 2005 by Abdo Consulting Group, Inc. International copyrights reserved in all countries. No part of this book may be reproduced in any form without written permission from the publisher.

Printed in the United States.

Edited by: Christy DeVillier
Contributing Editors: Matt Ray, Michael P. Goecke
Graphic Design: Maria Hosley
Image Research: Deborah Coldiron
Photographs: Corbis, Corel, Denise Esner, Mark Kostich, Minden Pictures, Photodisc

Library of Congress Cataloging-in-Publication Data

Murray, Julie, 1969-
  Elephants/Julie Murray.
      p. cm. — (Animal kingdom. Set II)
  Contents: Elephants — African elephants — Asian elephants — Their bodies — Trunks — Tusks — What they eat — Families — Babies.
  ISBN 1-59197-314-7
      1. Elephants—Juvenile literature. [1. Elephants.] I. Title.

QL737.P98 M867 2003
599.67—dc21

2002038562

Contents

Largest Land Animals

Elephants are famous for their trunks and **tusks**. The best-known **prehistoric** elephant is the woolly mammoth. It lived about 10,000 years ago. Today, elephants are the largest animals living on land.

The woolly mammoth was a prehistoric elephant.

Elephants are **mammals**. Mammals are born live instead of hatching from eggs. They use lungs to breathe air. Female mammals make milk in their bodies to feed their young. Wolves, apes, rats, whales, and people are mammals, too.

Kinds Of Elephants

There are two kinds of elephants: African elephants and Asian elephants. African elephants live in Africa. They live in forests and on grasslands.

Asian elephant

African elephant

Asian elephants live in Southeast Asia and India. They live in **tropical** forests and mountain forests.

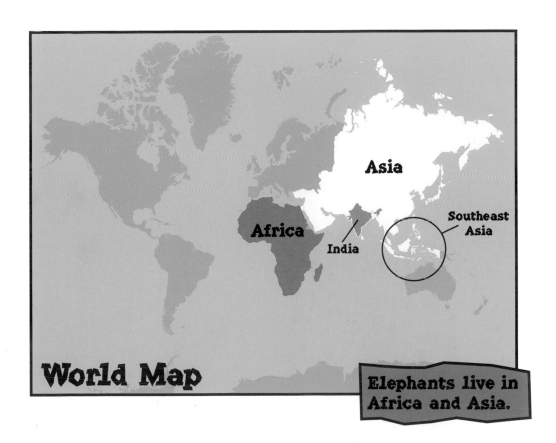

Asia

Africa

India

Southeast Asia

World Map

Elephants live in Africa and Asia.

African elephants are larger than Asian elephants. African elephants have longer **tusks** and bigger ears. Some people believe an African elephant's ears are shaped like Africa.

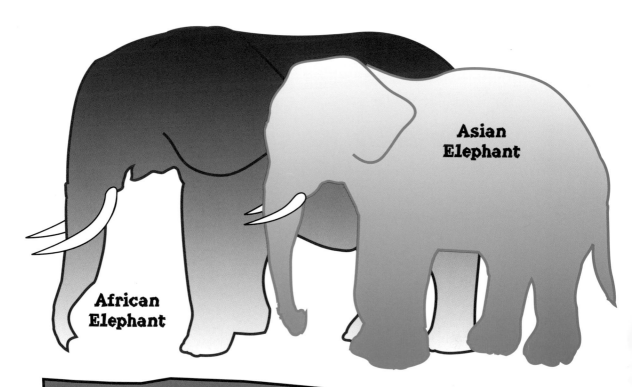

Asian Elephant

African Elephant

African elephants are larger than Asian elephants.

What They Look Like

Elephants have rough, thick skin. They walk on four strong legs. Elephants fan themselves with their large ears. This helps them stay cool.

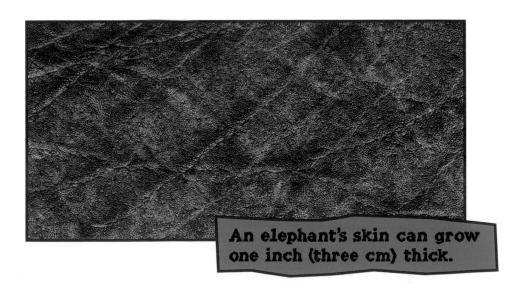

An elephant's skin can grow one inch (three cm) thick.

Male African elephants can grow to become as tall as 12 feet (4 m). Some are as heavy as a six-ton (five-t) school bus. Male Asian elephants grow to become about 10 feet (3 m) tall. Female elephants are smaller than the males.

Some elephants grow trunks as long as seven feet (two m). An African elephant has two "fingers" at the end of its trunk. An Asian elephant has one "finger." These special trunk "fingers" help elephants grab and pick up things.

Elephants can grab things with their special trunk "fingers."

One "Finger"

Asian Elephant

African Elephants

Two "Fingers"

Elephants grow long teeth called **tusks**. Female Asian elephants have small tusks that stay hidden. A male African elephant can grow tusks as long as six feet (two m).

Tusks are long teeth.

The Amazing Trunk

An elephant's trunk has thousands of muscles and no bones. It can move in many ways.

Elephants use their trunks all the time. They eat, drink, bathe, and smell with their trunks. An elephant's trunk is strong enough to lift heavy trees. They can also pick up tiny things with their trunk "fingers."

Herd Life

Adult female elephants are called cows. The cows live with their young in family **herds**. An older cow is the herd's leader. This leader is called the **matriarch**.

The matriarch leads the herd. She knows where to find food and water. The other cows learn from the matriarch.

Elephants live and travel in groups called herds.

Adult male elephants are called bulls. Bulls live alone or in a **herd** with other bulls.

Elephants do not stay in one place. They travel around looking for food. Sometimes, elephants must go far to find enough food.

Cow herds protect their young from danger.

Few animals hunt adult elephants. Baby elephants, or calves, must watch out for lions. A cow **herd** works together to protect their calves. Cows stand in a circle around their calves when danger is near.

Eating

Elephants eat plants. They eat berries, grass, leaves, roots, bark, fruit, and tree branches. An elephant can eat more than 300 pounds (136 kg) of food every day.

An elephant also needs a lot of water. It can drink 50 gallons (189 l) of water at one time. Sometimes elephants dig in the ground for water.

Elephants have four big teeth inside their mouths. They slide their teeth back and forth to break up food. This sliding wears down their teeth. Elephants grow new teeth to replace the worn ones. They can grow six sets of teeth.

Ivory Tusks

Elephant **tusks** are made of ivory. At one time, killing elephants for their ivory tusks was common. Today, this is against the law in many places. But elephants are still not safe from hunters. One way to help elephants is by never buying ivory.

Some elephants are killed for their ivory tusks.

Elephant Calves

Female elephants commonly have one calf at a time. A newborn calf weighs about 200 pounds (91 kg).

A baby elephant can walk within one hour after birth. It drinks its mother's milk. Calves begin eating plants after a few months. They will keep drinking milk for four years or longer.

A mother elephant bathes her calf.

It takes between 10 and 15 years for elephants to become adults. Adult males leave the family group. Adult females stay with their mother's **herd**. Elephants can live as long as 70 years.

A mother elephant and her calf.

Important Words

herd a large group of animals.

mammal most living things that belong to this special group have hair, give birth to live babies, and make milk to feed their babies.

matriarch the leader of an elephant herd of cows and young.

prehistoric describes anything that was around more than 5,500 years ago.

tropical weather that is warm and wet.

tusks large teeth that stick out of an animal's mouth.

Web Sites

To learn more about elephants, visit ABDO Publishing Company on the World Wide Web. Web sites about elephants are featured on our Book Links page. These links are routinely monitored and updated to provide the most current information available.

www.abdopub.com

Index